toot!

With love to everyone telling silly jokes at the Brereton Christmas table, past, present and future – C.B.

Thanks Santa for all the magical Christmases – S.J.

First published in Great Britain in 2022 by Red Shed, part of Farshore
An imprint of HarperCollins*Publishers*
1 London Bridge Street, London SE1 9GF
www.farshore.co.uk

HarperCollins*Publishers*
1st Floor, Watermarque Building, Ringsend Road,
Dublin 4, Ireland

Copyright © HarperCollins*Publishers* Limited 2022

Written by Catherine Brereton
Illustrations by Steve James

ISBN 978 0 00 852442 5
001
Printed and bound in the UK using 100% Renewable Electricity at CPI Group (UK) Ltd.

A CIP catalogue record for this title is available from the British Library.

MIX
Paper | Supporting responsible forestry
FSC™ C007454

This book is produced from independently certified FSC™ paper to ensure responsible forest management.

For more information visit: www.harpercollins.co.uk/green

CHRISTMAS WOULD YOU RATHER?

Written by Catherine Brereton
Illustrations by Steve James

RED SHED

Christmas is a wonderful time of year,
full of excitement, games and traditions,
presents, lots of food . . .
and plenty of silliness!

Do you like imagining silly situations
and making wacky choices?

Do you love spreading Christmas
cheer with hilarious jokes?

Want to impress your friends with some
amazing festive facts?

Read on for a Santa's sackful of hilarious
Would You Rather situations, laugh-out-loud
jokes and wild Christmas facts . . .

Would you rather play football dressed as **Santa** OR spend the school day covered in **tinsel** and **baubles?**

Would you rather have a carrot for a **nose** . . .

OR two Brussels sprouts for a **bottom?**

Would you rather smell like
a Brussels sprout **fart** for a month...

**OR eat one Brussels sprout
every day** for a year?

toot!

Supermarkets in the UK sell around
750 million sprouts every Christmas.

Brussels sprouts make your farts extra smelly! They contain a type of sugar that your body has trouble digesting, so this creates very smelly, eggy gases.

Would you rather have **fairy wings** but **NOT** be able to fly . . .

OR have **Rudolph's antlers** and **be able to fly?**

Would you rather be
a gingerbread person...

OR live in a **gingerbread house?**

The largest gingerbread house was over 3m tall. It was built in Texas, USA, and visitors could go inside it and meet Santa Claus!

Would you rather have a **penguin's head**...

OR reindeer feet?

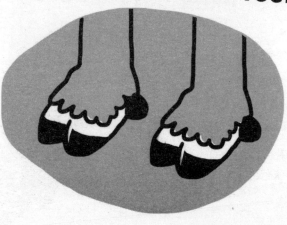

Would you rather **grow reindeer antlers**...

OR have **donkey ears** and a **tail?**

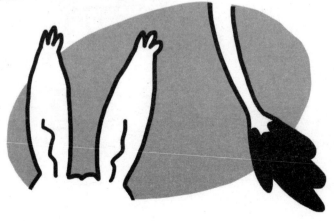

Would you rather go **ice skating** wearing just your swimming kit and skates . . .

OR wrap presents wearing ALL your hats, coats, scarves and mittens?

Would you rather sing 20 Christmas carols while **jumping on a trampoline** OR write 20 Christmassy words in **one minute?**

Mistletoe is a Christmassy word.
But did you know that it comes from
Old English words meaning 'poo' and
'twig'? Its twig-like stems grow on trees
after birds have eaten mistletoe berries,
sat on those trees and pooed out
the mistletoe seeds.

Would you rather be a judge at an elf talent show OR the referee in a reindeer sleigh race?

Reindeer hooves spread out like a sponge in summer. In winter they shrink and harden.

Reindeer have hairy hooves, which give them a good grip in the slippery snow – like snowshoes!

Would you rather wear a hat made of **Christmas pudding** ...

OR trousers made of chocolate?

Would you rather smell like **gingerbread** for a year OR look like a **gingerbread person** for a month?

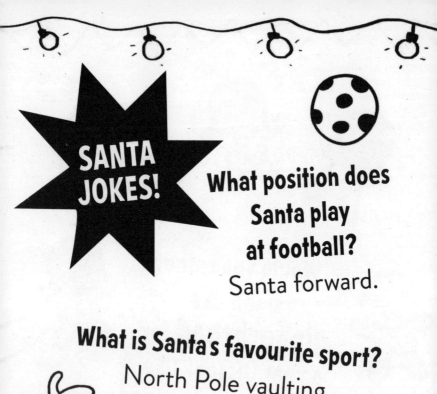

SANTA JOKES!

What position does Santa play at football?

Santa forward.

What is Santa's favourite sport?

North Pole vaulting.

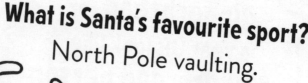

How does Santa ask Rudolph about the weather?

Is it going to rain, dear?

What says 'oh, oh, oh'?
Santa going backwards.

What goes red, white, red, white, red, white?
Santa rolling down a hill.

What do you get if you cross Santa with a duck?
A Christmas quacker.

Would you rather spend all day
tied to an elf...

OR challenge Santa to
a Christmas stocking race?

Astronauts don't pull Christmas crackers. If they did, the gunpowder that makes the bang would spark a blue-flamed blaze!

Some astronauts on the International Space Station eat Christmas dinner twice! Some have their festive feast on 25 December, while others have it on 7 January, which is Russian Christmas. Some like to join in both!

Would you rather eat a **pile** of **snowballs**...

OR wear **frozen underwear?**

Would you rather have a **snowball fight** with a snowman OR an **ice-skating race** with an elf?

In 2016, 7,681 people took part in a snowball fight in Saskatoon, Canada. That's a lot of snowballs!

Would you rather
drive a sleigh to school
OR **ride** there on a reindeer?

Reindeer fur has two layers
to keep the reindeer warm
in their snowy home.

Reindeer noses warm up the
air they breathe in, so it's no longer
frosty when it gets into their lungs.

Would you rather listen to 'White Christmas' all day every day for a month OR never listen to a Christmas song again?

...White Christmas...

'White Christmas' was recorded back in 1942 by long-ago legend Bing Crosby. It is the biggest-selling single of all time and has sold around 50 million copies!

'Jingle Bells' was the first song played in space.

Would you rather eat a 100-year-old Christmas cake...

A family in Michigan, USA, has a Christmas cake made by their great-great-grandmother over 140 years ago! The family stored it uneaten for most of that time, but tasted a small slice on a TV show in 2003.

OR gobble up enough raw carrots for all Santa's reindeer?

OR delivered them nicely wrapped but covered in **gravy**?

For Christmas dinner, would you rather have **Christmas pudding** made of dog food...

OR **yule log** full of real twigs?

For leftovers, would you rather have **turkey trifle**...

OR cold sprouts with custard?

Would you rather dress **Santa** in **fairy wings** OR a **reindeer onesie?**

Would you rather your **nose** could play 'Jingle Bells' OR you could grow a **real white beard** like Santa's?

SNOW JOKES!

What do snowmen like to do at the weekend?
Chill out.

What does a cyclist ride in the winter?
An icicle.

Where do snowmen go to dance?
A snowball.

Why was the snowman rummaging through a bag of carrots?
He was picking his nose.

What do snowmen wear on their heads?
Ice caps.

What's the difference between an ice cream and a polar bear?
If you don't know, then I'm never asking you to get me an ice cream!

Would you rather decorate 100 Christmas trees OR wrap 100 presents?

Decorating our homes in midwinter dates back before the first Christmas, to ancient Romans and other pagans. For them, evergreen plants, such as holly, ivy and mistletoe, were symbols of life in the depths of winter.

Would you rather go around with **mistletoe** on your head OR have **sleigh bells** on your fingers and toes?

Would you rather be
tickled by 20 elves...

OR snuggle up to a polar bear?

Would you rather be given 500 tins of pineapple OR a life-size chocolate coach?

Both of these are presents that Queen Elizabeth II has been given. In 1947, the government of Queensland, Australia, sent 500 tins of pineapple and in 2013 the chocolate company Mars gave her a chocolate coach.

Would you rather have
feet like skis OR arms like penguins' wings?

Would you rather it snowed
reindeer **poo** OR turkey **eggs**?

Would you rather your whole house **lit up** when you went to the **toilet** OR have your doorbell make a **farting noise?**

Some families' homes really light up the Christmas holidays. In 2014, a family in New York decorated the area outside their home with 601,736 lights.

Would you rather talk in cat noises all day on Christmas day OR try to teach your dog to bark Christmas carols?

A 2020 survey found that almost three-quarters of dog owners in the UK would be buying Christmas presents for their pooches.

In Iceland, a scary giant cat called the Yule Cat is said to eat little children if their parents haven't made them new clothes by Christmas Eve.

Would you rather decorate your tree with spiders OR cover it with robins?

In Ukraine, some people really do decorate their Christmas trees with spider and spider web decorations. This is after a traditional story in which a family was too poor to decorate their tree, so real spiders kindly decorated it with their webs on Christmas Eve.

Would you rather have hair made of tinsel OR gingerbread fingernails?

Would you rather have a **snowball fight** dressed **ONLY** in your **PE kit** **OR** go to **elf school?**

Would you rather go to school dressed in a **Santa suit** OR bake **Christmas cookies** for your whole class?

CAROL JOKES!

What's a dog's favourite carol?
Bark The Herald Angels Sing.

What carol might you sing in the desert?
O Camel Ye Faithful.

What do you get when you cross a Christmas song with a skunk?
Jingle Smells.

Why did the carol singers need a ladder?
To reach the high notes.

How do Christmas angels greet each other?
They say, 'Halo!'

Who gets the most Christmas party invitations?
Christmas Carol.

Would you rather a **polar bear** helped you with your homework . . .

A polar bear can smell its prey from more than a kilometre away.

OR a **penguin** helped you with your chores?

Penguins probably wouldn't be much help with cleaning. They make so much mess that it can be seen from space – they shoot streams of poo far away from their nests.

Would you rather make all the toys that Santa needs to deliver . . .

OR reply to ALL of Santa's letters that he has been sent?

In Finland there is an official Santa Claus Post Office – it receives half a million letters every year from children all over the world.

Would you rather look after a **reindeer** for the weekend OR sing 'Rudolph the Red-Nosed Reindeer' **non-stop** for a day?

Would you rather listen to someone playing Christmas songs on the **trombone** all day every day in December or eat **Christmas lunch** every day for a year?

Would you rather make your Christmas tree look like an **alien**...

OR your snowman look like a **monster?**

Do you want to build a snowman? In Sapporo, Japan, people really do. They build hundreds of snowmen during an ice festival every year.

Would you rather sing 'Jingle Bells' to a group of 1,000 people OR to one person whilst hanging upside down high up in the world's tallest Christmas tree?

The world's tallest cut Christmas tree went on display in Seattle, Washington, USA in 1950. It was 67.36m tall – that's about the height of 12 giraffes!

Jingle Bells
Jingle Bells

Would you rather decorate your Christmas tree with toilet paper OR cover your toilet with tinsel and baubles?

Would you rather drink lemonade out of an **elf hat** . . .

OR eat cereal out of one of **Santa's boots?**

Would you rather be given a machine that churns out Christmas chocolate for one whole day OR the world's biggest chocolate Santa?

In Germany, chocolate Santas are a big part of the Christmas treat traditions. Around 160 million chocolate Santas were made there in 2021.

ELF JOKES!

What kind of music do elves like to play while they work?
Wrap music.

What did Santa do when the elves kept misbehaving?
He gave them the sack.

What type of photos do Santa's helpers take?
Elfies.

What happens when you interrupt an elf reading a newspaper?
I don't know, but there'll be some crosswords!

What do elves learn first at school?
The elf-abet.

What do you call an elf with lots of money?
Welfy.

Would you rather have a **bath** with a **penguin OR run a race** against a **turkey?**

Turkeys can run FAST. They reach speeds of up to 40km/h – a lot faster than the quickest sprinter in your school, and nearly as fast as the world's fastest human sprinter at top speed!

Would you rather have a present-wrapping **robot** OR a **toaster** that plays Christmas carols?

Would you rather stay in an
ice hotel where **Santa's elves**
are having a noisy party
OR sleep in a barn with
ALL of **Santa's reindeer?**

Would you rather your bedroom smelled like **sprouts** cooking OR reindeer **poo**?

Would you rather wash your hair with **gravy** . . .

OR use Christmas **trifle** as a body lotion?

Would you rather **brush** a donkey's teeth OR **muck out** a donkey's stable?

Would you rather sleep in a **manger** OR read a book while perched up a **Christmas tree?**

Nativity scenes usually feature a familiar list of figures: Mary, Joseph, baby Jesus, shepherds, angels, the wise men and various animals. But in some parts of Spain and France there is also a little man with his trousers down, called *El Caganer* or 'the pooper'!

Would you rather make a snowman out of **mashed potato OR squirty cream?**

Movie snow is often made out of mashed potato! Well, nearly. Fake snow is made of flakes of potato. When it's wet, it has a mashed potato-like consistency, which is both sticky and biodegradable.

Would you rather **balance** a **mince pie** on your head for five minutes OR **decorate** 20 **Christmas cookies** in one minute?

Would you rather have your Christmas presents delivered by a **goat**...

Every Christmas in Sweden, many towns and cities have a large straw statue of the Yule Goat. There are lots of traditions based around it – one is the idea that it brings Christmas gifts.

OR your cards delivered by a **robin?**

Robins are popular birds on Christmas cards. In Victorian England, postmen wore red uniforms and were nicknamed robins – just when Christmas cards were becoming popular. So robins really did deliver the Christmas post!

Would you rather sing in your school carol concert dressed in **football kit** OR go to a ballet class dressed as a **snowman**?

Would you rather balance
12 **baubles** on your head OR tie your
coat and shoelaces with **tinsel?**

ANIMAL JOKES!

What do you do when you arrive at a reindeer's house?
Ring the deer-bell.

What do you call a reindeer with bad manners?
Rude-olph.

Why was Rudolph disappointed with his school test results?
Because he went down in history.

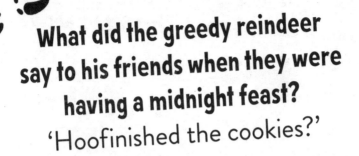

What did the greedy reindeer say to his friends when they were having a midnight feast?
'Hoofinished the cookies?'

Which animals are best for writing Christmas cards?
Pen-guins.

Who delivers Christmas presents to baby sharks?
Santa Jaws.

Would you rather star in
a Christmas movie OR sing
on a number one Christmas song?

Would you rather your Christmas
presents came alive OR your
Christmas sweets started dancing?

The Nutcracker is a famous ballet. It tells the story of Clara. One Christmas Eve, her toys come to life. She meets an army of mice and live toy soldiers, and her nutcracker doll is transformed into a handsome prince. They travel to a snowy fairyland where they meet dancing flowers and sweets.

Would you rather build a **den** in the snow OR take a **dip** in an **icy sea?**

Many seaside towns around the UK have a tradition of Christmas Day or Boxing Day dips. Brave swimmers take a quick plunge in the cold water – for charity, in fancy dress or just for fun!